# ANGER MANAGEMENT

*A Psychologist's Guide to Master Your Emotions, Identify & Control Anger To Ultimately Take Back Your Life*

KATHERINE CHAMBERS

# TABLE OF CONTENTS

# INTRODUCTION

"Holding onto anger is like grasping a hot coal with the intent of throwing it at someone else; you are the one who gets burned"

(Buddha)

Imagine a world of complete and utter harmony, satisfaction and sheer bliss. Now think of your life. It's somewhat different right? The thing is, that's totally OK. Anger, fear and frustration are as much a part of the human experience as any of the above feelings of peace and well-being. It's an inescapably fact.

The key is identifying the causes of your anger, to fully recognize it and take responsibility for it. To see it for what it is, an outward expression of some deeper cognitive dissonance in your mind. When you can do that you can go about constructively reducing it's impact on your life in a negative fashion, and even direct the energy it brings to the surface into more positive avenues.

That is really what anger management is all about:

1. Identifying the underlying causes of your frustrations

2. Dealing with these issues directly until they no longer have an affect over you

1

I'm not saying that this is an easy process by any means, it is not. It's a journey like every other psychological self-development path you will find yourself on. But like any other, it will be well worth the time and effort you will put into it.

My aim for this book is to both layout the principles and concepts behind the feelings of anger and rage, but more importantly to give you the knowledge and tools to better deal with them when they arise. To lessen the impact they have on your life in an adverse manner, and even ways to make them work in your favor.

The following chapters will show you just that, so approach this with a fresh and open mind and hopefully you will gain some insights to ultimately lead a more harmonious life going forward.

## My Credentials

Before we get into the ins and outs of anger management it's probably a good idea for me to explain exactly who I am, and why you should even bother listening to me in the first place. Yes I have the undergraduate and master's degree in psychology from Stanford, but my main focus over the past 15 years or so has been on the practical elements of the discipline. I wouldn't ever call myself a "Self-Help Guru" but I do focus much more on the results of these principles in the real world compared to my previous life of studying endless research papers on the academic side of the subject.

I use what I have learnt and observe the behavior and psychological patterns of other successful people in life to pin point exactly what it is they are doing to elicit the results they are achieving. There are common patterns to these people and behaviors if you know how to spot them. Luckily for you even if you don't, I have spent the past 2 decades working this stuff out for you. I have dedicated my 40's to documenting both the rationale behind the most important psychological mindsets as well as the practical advice on how to cultivate the ability to use them to your benefit in the real world.

It all started when I was just a young girl growing up on the east coast, I was a very observant kid. I was the youngest of four in our family which was fine with me as I would get to watch my older sister and brothers in action. Watch for their actions and behaviors, their successes and failures as almost a dry run for what I should be doing.

This continued through high school and into college, I luckily had a very active and ambitious peer group, it's hard not to when you live on the Stanford campus. I played a high level of lacrosse as well as track and field whilst at university so got to view the psychology of team/individual sports as well as in academia.

However it's not since leaving college life and living in the real world that I have really developed a taste for the subjects I once studied. It's all well and good reading the intricacies of psychological theories from the comfort of your dorm room or library, but it's not until you have to put these theories to the test in life in general do you really understand how they work. It's not until you have to make your way in business, within a career, build a family for yourself do you really understand the impact your mindset has to your overall success.

For me that has been building a multi-six figure consulting business and now a family of my own. But I am not here to blow my own horn or preach in anyway, nobody needs that. What I will do is put things into perspective, what I know to be true from the science behind these principles combined with my experience in the real world. I have made many mistakes along the way and will point out these pitfalls for you.

So why am I such an expert on anger management? As I mentioned, I studied a wide range of topics within the field of psychology and neuroscience whilst at college which formed my base understanding, but I have since picked up many critical skill sets whilst building a family and career of my own. Everything from managing my personal and business relationships to my own mental state. Everything has been a learning curve and one which has taken deep emotional understanding and soul searching at times.

The real world is about problem solving, it's about rapport building with others and creating harmony within yourself. However sometimes these things can go awry, they can start to frustrate you to the point of anger or even rage. As I mentioned in the open remarks to this book, this is not something to be ashamed of, it's a normal aspect of life. The key is in dealing with these tenancies and managing these emotions to the best effect.

So now that you know a little more about me, let's dive in. The following chapters will teach you everything you need to know in order to become proficient at spotting your own personal pain points. But ultimately provide you with the tools and knowledge on how to deal with them in the future.

A lot of this involves identifying the underlying issues you have and the triggers which set these episodes off. So make sure you are as open and honest with yourself when going through this process. I promise you it will be worth it.

# PART 1

# A BASIC UNDERSTANDING OF ANGER MANAGEMENT PRINCIPLES

# CHAPTER 1

# BIOCHEMISTRY BEHIND ANGER

While some may think that anger is merely an emotion that is triggered by a random event. The truth is, there is always an underlying cause behind it. In fact, certain things happen within the human body which in turn leads to the emotion of anger. At the same time, different things will happen to the human body once anger envelopes you.

Anger can trigger both acute and chronic changes in the human body, and some of these changes may have adverse effects to trigger life-altering events. An in-depth look at the biochemistry and physiology behind anger can help uncover an intricate interplay within the human body. Such interplay offers an explanation on why people become angry, why some people get more easily angered than others, and provides an insight on the potential solutions to anger, among other questions.

Emotions in general are a joint experience by the mind and body. While most people think that anger "is all in the mind", the body certainly has a say in this process. Again, just like with other emotions, the physiological events that happen before, during, and after we become angry are complex, with most of these events interplaying with one another.

Just like with practically all emotions, it all starts in the brain. To be more specific, it starts at the amygdala, a component of the limbic system located in the basal ganglia. A pair of almond-shaped structures, the amygdala plays an important role in memories, and partly for identifying potential threats to our well-being. These memories would then trigger the emergence of emotions, which would subsequently be transmitted to the cerebral cortex for processing. Basically, such emotions are protective by nature; they are triggered to create an appropriate response to perceived threats to our well-being.

When you are angry, different hormones are released from your body, which causes a wide range of physiological changes. The most prominent hormone produced during outbursts of anger are catecholamines such as epinephrine and norepinephrine. Produced by the adrenal glands during stressful situations, it helps the human body appropriately cope with stressful situations.

Your blood pressure rises and your blood vessels dilate, causing increased blood flow to all parts of your body. Heart rate and respiratory rate both increase, ensuring that your body has more than enough supply of oxygen and energy. Your mind also becomes more "locked in", placing your focus towards the cause of your aggression. Such processes are responsible for the marked changes in your physical and mental state during bursts of anger.

Of course, an angry state cannot be sustained indefinitely. After all, prolonged states of anger can be damaging to your health, as evidenced during acute and chronic stress disorders.

Eventually, your body needs to revert to its "normal state". After a burst of anger, your body winds down, returning all physiological functions back to their usual baseline states. It usually takes some time before catecholamine levels subside. The aroused state caused by anger usually lasts moments if you are lucky, and hours if you are not.

What's more, while in this cool-down state, our anger threshold becomes lower, meaning we get angry more quickly. It is no coincidence why it doesn't take much to anger people who are constantly angry. It's their default sate of mind.

On a related note, there is also a physiologic explanation why we seem to not remember much about our anger outbursts. This is because when the brain is too aroused (such as in states of extreme emotion such as anger outbursts), processing memories becomes very difficult.

Aside from the reduced ability to process memories, increased levels of arousal make it difficult to concentrate. The combination of these 2 effects make it difficult to remember the details of your worst anger outbursts. So, do you remember every detail of the last time you become extremely angry? If you do, the memory tends to be fuzzier than usual.

While it is not easy to stay under control when you are angry, it is still doable. This is made possible by our cerebral cortex. As I mentioned previously, the amygdala communicates with the cerebral cortex to determine the most appropriate plan of action during a stressful situation.

The prefrontal cortex of your cerebrum is mainly responsible for controlling your judgment, it's the part of the brain involved with rationalization and advanced cognition of all kinds. It can shut off all emotions, keeping you under control even during bursts of extreme emotion. This function allows you to control your anger, and on occasions even use it to your advantage.

Balancing the actions of the amygdala and prefrontal cortex is at the heart of a lot of principles of anger management. During bursts of anger, these 2 parts of your brain go on a virtual tug-of-war. While the amygdala is pushing you to go over the edge and act based on instinct, your prefrontal cortex is trying to keep things under control and maintain a rational state of mind.

Learning how to master this delicate balance has been the subject of most emotional programs. You would want your emotions to take your performance to the next level, but not at the cost of doing irrational things.

# CHAPTER 2

# WHAT ACTUALLY CAUSES ANGER?

"Anger is nothing more than an outward expression of hurt, fear and frustration"

(Phil McGraw)

Anger is an emotion experienced by everyone at different stages of their lives and to varying degrees, it's inescapable. From a seemingly benign annoyance to a full-blown outrage, people experience anger accordingly and express it in a myriad of ways. One of the ways to understand anger is to take a closer look on what causes it to begin with.

So, what is the real cause of anger? There are so many ways to answer this question, different forms of stimuli anger people, but its always a result of some form of underlying issue. This chapter will take a closer look at the different causes and why people get angry as a result of these "triggers".

From a psychological perspective, anger is considered a natural reaction to pain. This pain is not limited to the physical, but it can also be caused by emotional factors. It does not matter what triggers this pain; anger is triggered by an experience that can be defined as painful or unpleasant. It is for this reason that anger is considered as a "secondhand emotion", an emotion caused by something else (in this case, pain).

Anger is also considered as a social emotion, an emotion that has a direct target. When you experience anger, it is more often targeted towards someone or something. Then more often then not, this target ends up enduring the lion share of your outburst.

People can end up getting angry for all kinds of reasons. As mentioned earlier, anger as an emotion is rarely spontaneous, it is usually predicated on some underlying discomfort or dissonance in the persons mind. However there will certainly be a trigger to set off an angered response in the moment.

It must be noted that your anger may be caused by someone or something else. With that out of the way, the next list contains some of the most common reasons why a person can get angry. Do you get mad because of any of these common tendencies?

## 1. Anger is a means to cope with pain

People get hurt physically, mentally, and emotionally all the time. They tend to do different things to deal with this pain. One of the more common ways people deal with the pains they experience is through anger. Anger is used to either mask the pain they are feeling or channel it out to someone or something else. It is common for angry people to lash out just to "let off steam".

It also becomes a means for letting out the pain they are feeling, even if its temporary. It's no surprise that people dealing with problems are the ones most prone to bursts of anger, it's a cathartic release for them but as we will see later on, there are much healthier and better ways of doing this.

## 2. Anger is a response to one's interpretation of things

People have different ways of interpreting the situations which are going on around them. When people interpret something and have found it to be unpleasant, it almost always results in a reactionary emotion such as anger.

From there, it is up to the person how they are going to express this emotion (this will be discussed in greater depth later). There are different ways people express their anger, but their reaction is almost always a product of how they interpret a specific situation they have found themselves in.

## 3. Anger is a way to get even

Some people may have experienced bad things in the past. Others may even still be experiencing them today. As a means for dealing with these unpleasant situations they often resort to bursts of anger, often directed to another person. Their anger is often triggered by desires of revenge, which may or may not be expressed towards the one they believed caused their pain to begin with.

It has been proven that people who have dealt with negative experiences in the past I.e. hardship, abuse and failures are more prone to anger management issues in the future, as well as related behaviors such as inappropriate aggression and bullying.

## 4. Anger is used to hide one's emotions and vulnerabilities

Some people make it a point to conceal their real emotions for one reason or another. Some do it because they are pretending that they are somebody who they are not. Others do it because they are trying to mask their own weaknesses.

Whatever it may be, anger is usually an emotion expressed to show strength and mask whatever insecurities they have. They use hostility to protect themselves against others who might hurt them, or at least deter them from doing so. Vulnerable people are also more aggressive by nature, as they tend to overcompensate and resort to prejudiced responses.

## 5. Anger is a way to justify acts that are otherwise wrong

Anger is a commonly used alibi by some people to justify actions that would otherwise be considered wrong or inappropriate. They perform inappropriate acts and then say that they did it because they were angry. On paper, it is an effective cop-out that enables people to not take responsibility for their actions, or worse to condone this behavior as being acceptable.

"I did what I did because they made me angry." How many times have you heard this refrain, whether from others or even from yourself? Anger creates a feeling of righteousness and moral superiority, a feeling that can could quash a persons inner demons.

But as we have seen already, anger in general is never a result of complete spontaneity. It is almost always rooted into something much deeper. Regardless of the reason for your anger, it is born out of some underlying issue you haven't yet dealt with.

Addressing the reasons for your anger lies in the heart of the principles and techniques used in all anger management programs. As such, it is important that you find the reasons why you get mad and you make an appropriate response towards it. This will help you better deal with your rage and manage the potentially negative effects they may be causing you.

# CHAPTER 3

# THE COMMON EFFECTS OF ANGER

"Nobody makes you angry. You decide to use anger as a response"

(Brain Tracey)

As I have mentioned, I used to study these psychological concepts in-depth, but you don't have to be a master in psychology to know that the effects of anger in your life are real. You simply have to reflect on your moments of anger, regardless of the reason or the scale of your reaction. Looking back at those moments, you might be surprised at how you dealt with the situation.

There could be moments when your anger caused you to behave in a completely different manner, something beyond your understanding. This isn't something to beat yourself up about, it's a natural occurrence which happens to everyone at some stage. However it's about assessing the causes and common effects of these situations when they do arise.

# How People Express Anger

People express anger in many different ways, and they do it both consciously and unconsciously. Here are some of the most common ways in which people express their emotional anguish:

## 1. Some don't express it at all

Some people get angry, but they never really express it outwardly. A lot of people do not express their anger because of the awareness that something bad might happen should they let it out. Instead, they try t0 get it pent-up inside.

While such actions are borderline admirable, and this can work in certain instances, there are real risks associated with the non-expression of rage. Unexpressed anger can lead to a number of health problems (more on this later). It can also lead to the development of bad behavior and habits such as hostility and cynicism. Some may think it's a compromise and that instead of being outwardly angry, they bottle up inside, but such practices can lead to its own spectrum of problems.

## 2. Some express their anger physically

Inflicting physical pain to one's self or others is one of the most overt and scariest aspects of ill-managed anger.

Physical aggression falls into two categories by and large: aggression against people and aggression against objects. Aggression against other people often results in assaulting them with the use of their own hands or weapons including punching, slapping, pushing etc. The latter is defined as aggression expressed against other random physical objects. Examples of these include but not limited to throwing objects, banging walls and slamming doors.

Physical expressions of anger cause tangible damages, and can be especially traumatic for anyone who experiences or even witnesses it.

### 3. Some express their anger verbally

Much has been said about physical abuse, but verbal abuse is one of the most underrated yet destructive forms of manifesting anger. People verbally express their anger in different ways, with virtually all of them causing hurtful effects.

People may raise their voice, use profanity, insult, embarrass, and even threaten the people they are talking to. Verbal abuse may happen only as a one-time event, but there are many cases wherein verbal abuse happens repeatedly over a long period of time. When expressed verbally, anger can still cause very adverse effects to the one who receives it.

### 4. Some express their anger indirectly

Some people make it a point to not express their anger directly for different reasons. Some do it out of fear of the person they are mad at, or out of the knowledge that expressing one's anger directly does not present a good look. As such, they express their anger in an indirect manner.

They can show it by nonverbal shows of indirect aggression such as angry stares, dismissiveness, and purposeful ignoring. There are others who choose to go the passive-aggressive route, such as sulking, performing tasks poorly on purpose, and exhibiting poor body language. At times, they would just confide their frustrations to others as a substitute to confronting their source of anger.

## 5. Some express their anger to others

Displaced anger is one of the most common means in which it is expressed. You can see this phenomenon virtually everywhere. Often, people cannot overtly express their anger to someone or something in the moment.

They instead choose to vent this frustration to someone else, most commonly to another person in a different setting. The most common victims of displaced anger include children, subordinates at work, or friends. Displaced anger can be expressed in a wide variety of ways, including but not limited to the earlier examples mentioned.

## 6. Some change their behaviors

Anger is a powerful emotion that can completely shape a person in extreme circumstances. In response to anger, some undergo several behavioral changes. Some of them subside once the feelings of anger go away, while other behavioral changes stick with them for long periods of time.

The most common behavioral change observed in angry people is that they become more aggressive, often at the cost of more logical thinking. Others build a wall of resentment and bad feelings, making it difficult for others to reach out to them. There are also people who become avoidant to deflect these bad feelings.

While there are situations wherein anger is indeed beneficial (more on this later), in most cases, the effects of anger end up adversely affecting everyone involved. In fact, more often then not, whether in its acute or chronic form, expressed or otherwise, anger just hurts more than it helps.

## Effects of Anger

Frustration in essence causes you to lose sight of what's important, makes you commit mistakes you otherwise wouldn't when you're feeling calm. It destroys relationships and other social ties, causes your health and well-being to take a nosedive, and overall just makes you miserable.

Here are some of the unhealthy effects of anger in greater detail.

### 1. Anger affects your physical health

Most people take this concept way too lightly, especially in their younger years. But anger can definitely compromise your health if you let it get out of hand. During a sudden burst of anger, you may experience multiple changes in your physiological functions, which may make you more prone to specific diseases (over time).

For example, the sudden surge of blood pressure can make you prone to acute cardiovascular events such as heart attacks, strokes, and ruptured blood vessels. Also, chronic anger creates a constellation of more silent but equally destructive effects to your health. Anger sustained over a long period of time is a risk factor associated to many life-threatening diseases as its affects cause high levels of stress inside the body.

## 2. Anger affects your mental health

Being in a constant state of rage has a detrimental effect on your mental health too. Being angry can cause damage to your self-esteem. This is because the expression of anger may lead to feelings of guilt, remorse, and shame after the fact.

Anger also teaches you to develop certain behaviors to adapt, with some of them ending up being maladaptive ones. However, even without anger, such problems do not go away and may even get worse. In addition to this, some of the physical effects of anger (especially difficulty in sleeping) may cause impaired cognitive function compounding any pre-existing mental conditions a person may have.

Lastly, sustained anger coupled with unresolved personal issues can make a person more prone to developing mental health problems in general.

## 3. Anger can adversely affect your daily functioning

Some would say that being angry can help raise the level of your daily functioning by encouraging productivity. However, the risk of having the completely opposite effect is also very much real. It's a very fine line to tread and overstepping it can adversely affect your daily functioning in a wide variety of ways.

Your anger may distract you from doing what you need to do, resulting in sloppy performance. Also, anger may prevent you from performing to the best of your abilities by narrowing your focus too much, which can prove to be the difference between success and failure in many situations. As I touched upon above, anger can make you sick both literally and figuratively if you are not careful, reducing your productivity in any daily activity as a result.

## 4. Anger leads to impaired decision making

Anyone who has ever gotten extremely angry knows how hard it is to make decisions in this state. Even though the decision-making faculties of your brain are still fully functional, all of the raging hormones and pent-up emotions make it quite difficult to process everything in a logical manner. The "fight or flight" central nervous system responses have kicked in.

At the same time, your rage provides a major source of distraction as it would basically dictate that you make your choices to satisfy your anger. Impaired decision making puts you at risk of creating more problems moving forward. The famous quote "never make important decisions when you're mad" rings so true here.

## 5. Anger compromises social ties

Anger is one emotion which is directly linked to the destruction of social ties at all levels. Anger can harm relationships in so many ways. Firstly, a hostile attitude is not an ideal trait to have if you want to build strong and meaningful relationships. Secondly, people who are dealing with anger management problems are less compassionate, intimate, and kind to the people they are connecting with.

Another aspect to consider here is that issues with anger make it difficult for people to form relevant relationships to begin with. They find it difficult to interact with other people, and other people tend to be put off by their hostile attitude from the get go. It's a vicious circle which is hard to break if a change in attitude is not made.

## 6. Anger leads to more anger

This is the thing about keeping an angry state of mind; anger can sometimes lead to more anger. An angry mood has a way of perpetuating itself; if the stimulus for your rage continues to stay, there's a good chance for the anger to keep lingering (and compounding). What's more, their cynicism and their compromised view in life makes it hard for the person to appreciate the things in their life, which in turn can lead to more anger and frustration.

Until the person finds a resolution to the issues that are bothering him/her, there's a good chance that the anger will stay and possibly even grow. People have different ways of expressing this dissatisfaction with the world. However, most of the time, the result remains the same: adverse, hostile, violent, or even fatal.

Anger that is not properly addressed can end up reducing a person's quality of life immensely. Hence, it is important that any anger management issues must be brought to light. The first step in resolving this issue is to acknowledge that there's a problem needed to be resolved. This is where taking responsibility of your anger comes into the picture.

# CHAPTER 4

# DON'T TAKE IT PERSONAL - TAKING RESPONSIBILITY FOR YOUR EMOTIONS

"He who controls his own thoughts , controls his own destiny"

(Ross Arntson)

People all to frequently use the excuse that they only behaved in the way they have done or acted differently to how they normal would due to the fact they were angry. Some even attribute it to "impulsive anger". Whilst it is not always easy to control your rage on a moment to moment basis, and people can do some extreme things when they are angry. However it is never an excuse to do negative things just because of anger alone, or any other intense emotion for that matter.

You have to learn to control your temper, that is the duty of all adults. If you cannot control this intense emotion, you should take responsibility for the emotion, as well as the potential consequences of your actions. An important part of personal responsibility is to be responsible for one's behaviors and feelings, whether they may be good or bad. Never blame impulsive behavior to justify how you act and behave.

I am not saying that you need to become a sterile robot, that is impossible. Human beings are emotional creatures by nature. However you do have the choice on how you react to these impulses when they arise. As I mentioned earlier, a person is performing a constant tug-of-war between the older primitive parts of the brain such as the amygdala, and the newer more rational prefrontal cortexes.

I describe the influence of our primitive limbic system and the effects it exhibits over our emotional state at length in other books, but I will copy a passage here to describe more clearly what I mean. It's taken from a chapter within *Emotional Intelligence: A Psychologist's Guide* called "Living Our Limbic Legacy":

## The Old Mammalian Brain

"However what isn't in doubt is the development and influence of the limbic system on our psychological behaviors when it comes to emotional intelligence influences brought about by human interaction. Basically any thought that originates in the spinal cord must pass through the "rational" part of the brain, the frontal cortexes in order to be rationalized, conceptualized and understood.

However before it reaches these structures a thought must pass through the limbic system, the more primitive part of the brain where they become "emotionally charged" meaning that we have an emotional reaction to an event before the complex cognitive prefrontal lobe can engage and make sense of it.

"The emotional brain responds to an event more quickly than the thinking brain"

(Daniel Goleman)

The limbic system isn't a single structure within the brain but rather a set of structures which are located on both sides of the thalamus and positioned just below the cerebrum. It is sometimes referred to as the paleomammalian cortex or the "old mammalian brain" owing to the time period in which it evolved within us.

Essentially these were the first structures that set us apart from our reptilian ancestors, an addition and upgrade of hardware to the primitive structures of the archipallium which is comprised of the brain stem, medulla, cerebellum and oldest basal nuclei. These structures are primarily concerned with just the base sensory organs and simple motor functions, the starting point of any complex organism.

But the limbic system can do much more than this, as a system it supports a host of other functions including emotional regulation, long-term memory capability, ambition and all types of motivational behavior in general. It is basically the driving seat of our emotion center, as the structures heavily influence the endocrine system which intern regulates the dopermaneric pleasure responses to natural and recreational 'highs' alike.

The limbic system also has heavy input on the autonomic nervous system which mediates the 'fight or flight' response within us which can have many knock-on effects to our emotional state as well. However all of these elements are still very base and primitive components with regards to the human biological make-up but which still affect our day-to-day lives in a big way even today.

As much as we try to escape this ancestral legacy with the development of the outer neocortexes which provides the machinery that primes us for complex decision making cognition, we are constantly held back by an undersized prefrontal lobe and over powering limbic system. Don't get me wrong, I would certainly rather live in a world that allowed for the emotions of love, connection and compassion which the limbic system affords, but the flip side of this is fear, jealously and aggression which is elicited from these primal centers in exactly the same way.

Now you might be wondering what exactly this has to do with emotional intelligence and the answer is in a monumental way. Essentially what you are doing when you are attempting to develop E.I. is foster the positive parts of this limbic system activity i.e. bonding, rapport building and compassion whilst downplaying the negative side such as fear, anxiety and anger.

Emotional intelligence also comes heavily into play when trying to read someone to develop the social awareness aspects of E.I. which are crucial. What you are actually attempting to do is read the emotional cues the other person is giving away. The physiological changes the body produces naturally, unconsciously and automatically which is almost impossible to mask. This may include getting flush in the face when embarrassed or perspiring when nervous. Trying to control the volume and tonality of the voice when angry or fidgety movements of the body when anxious, it's very difficult to do.

These physiological responses were once highly useful as they were the only means for us to communicate what we were thinking or feeling. They are still very relevant even in today's world of modern speech with regards to conveying emotion, and this can certainly work in your favor when developing the social E.I. you are looking for.

Essentially emotional intelligence requires very effective symbiosis and communication between the newer wet wear of the rational brain with older more primitive emotional structures of the limbic system. There is a term for this communicative ability and brain development in general which neuroscientists refer to a "neuroplasticity". It's basically the process of forming new neural pathways and connections in the brain in response to new learning.

Using certain strategies to develop your own E.Q. levels is no different. When performing these learning techniques you are strengthening the billions of microscopic neuron pathways lining the road between the old emotional centers and the newer rational structures. This also allows for these pathways to branch out, much like a tree to form new connections with surrounding cells again improving overall capacity and cognitive ability. It has been estimated that a single cell can grow up to 15,000 new connections with its surrounding neighbors.

This process essentially further increases the rate of the positive feedback loops and ensures that like anything else which is practiced consistently and over time, it becomes habitual in nature and easier to perform in the future. Emotional intelligence is therefore a skill which is learned like any other"

So as you can see there is clear separation between the "Thinker" and "Feeler" within every person and they can often pull in very different directions. This is what ultimately leaves some people open to angry behavior, if the above two are not congruently aligned.

Your feelings compel you to do things from within, while your thoughts will compel you to do things from without. This is an important distinction to make because the freedom of being able to choose rather than being compelled to do things is a huge difference.

Making a choice is always internal, it's always up to the individual if he/she will do something or not. Most people take into consideration the consequences of their actions and what others will think of them, before making a choice or a decision. There is a difference between believing that you need to do something, and in choosing things based on what's truly important.

## Blaming Others

It is also a common refrain for people to blame a negative emotional reaction towards someone else. You may often say that your hurt feelings and your subsequent reaction is another person's fault, because of the hurtful things they have done to you.

However, no matter how bad this behavior is perceived to be, ultimately it is you who will decide what to react to and how to react. There will be situations and stimuli that trigger this response from you. Identifying them and managing how you would react towards such a trigger is one of the keys to managing anger. But the first step is always knowing that such triggers exist and that you own up to them.

There are multiple benefits of taking responsibility for your anger. The first reason is because it breaks the vicious cycle of "keeping score" of wrongs committed against you. One of the most common reasons why anger lingers is because people tend to keep a mental note of such transgressions, which keeps the intense feelings of anger fueled.

You need to take note that even when the subject of your anger, may it be your spouse, your child, your friend, your relative, your colleague, or someone you don't even know, may be the one at fault, you are still responsible for your own behavior and reaction. It is also not a good idea to make their mistakes your excuse to express your anger.

Taking responsibility for your feelings also gives you the incentive to control your behavior more effectively and keep a respectful approach all of the time. It takes a lot of class and discipline to maintain your composure even when things are not going your way, even if you do not like what you are seeing.

Knowing that you don't have the "moral leverage" to get angry makes you look for ways to improve how you react in such situations. When you prioritize controlling your behavior over reacting to whatever's going on around you, you gain better control of your anger and your emotions in general.

Taking responsibility of your anger also helps in developing confidence and self-esteem. A pathological lack of self-esteem is one of the most common reasons for anger management issues, as well as other common attitude problems.

When you can manage your behavior, and overcome the usual triggers that may cause you to "lose it", it adds to your confidence.

As you start building your confidence, it becomes easier to handle all kinds of adverse situations. An improved confidence enhanced by the ability to manage anger better will help you in just about every aspect of life.

# CHAPTER 5

# ANGER MANAGEMENT AS A CONCEPT

"We cling to the justifications of our anger with a desperate stubbornness, because otherwise we would have to deal with the overwhelming pain that underlies it"

(Greg Bacr)

Anger management is defined as a program designed to prevent and control anger. These programs consider such feelings to be emotionally rooted to an identifiable cause. By approaching this cause, anger can be controlled or at least minimized.

The causes of anger were already discussed in earlier chapters, as well as its effects. Whilst it is mainly psycho-therapeutic in nature, it is now considered as a multi-disciplinary practice. Among the professionals that may be involved in the initiation of anger management programs include psychologists, physicians, social workers, and occupational therapists.

While it is considered as a normal human emotion, people are all to aware of the potentially destructive effects of anger. In fact, the negative effects of anger have been well documented throughout history, and are a common topic in different schools of thought, from philosophy to religion. Given this level of awareness, people throughout history have searched for ways to minimize the destructive effects of such behavior. From avoidance of provocative situations to prayers, people from the ancient times were aware of the need to effectively control anger.

Anger management as a therapeutic method has mainly been developed through the 20th century though. Anger management is considered as a product of research and other endeavors by psychologists. In the 1970s, anger management interventions based on classical psychotherapy methods were already widely used. Soon after, cognitive behavioral therapy, a technique mainly used for treating anxiety disorders, was deemed to be an effective treatment for managing anger. Other psychological techniques were developed to address both anger/rage and its subsequent effects.

There are two different approaches that may be utilized in an anger management program. The first way to go about it is a do-it-yourself approach. The alternative is to get the help of a professional, such as a counselor or a psychotherapist. These two approaches need not be mutually exclusive, however, and a combination of self-help and professional guidance is seen to provide the greatest benefit.

Both of these approaches and their respective advantages will be talked about in the second part of this book. For now, it's important for you to know that both approaches can work for you and may actually be beneficial in achieving your desired goals depending on your case.

Anger management programs usually run within a specific time frame, with the prescribed length of treatment mainly dependent on the severity of the patient's condition and how well they respond to the program. A set number of sessions may be prescribed, depending on the program given for the patient. Professionals from different disciplines may work with the patient in an aim to resolve their issues.

Therapies can be done on a 1-on-1 setting, or it can be done within a group of people dealing with similar problems.

What are the goals of undergoing anger management? Of course, the general goal is to be able to keep one's anger under control. While it can be argued that anger cannot be totally suppressed, there is a way for this emotion to be deployed in a healthier manner.

Such programs help in identifying factors that cause people to get angry in the first place, such as failures, frustrations, and fears. After identifying the potential causes, a program can then be created to resolve or at least regulate them. Such programs are also designed to control one's response to anger, so that anger related problems can be effectively avoided.

It is important to note that anger management is there to help a person overcome their anger related issues. However, such programs are more than just that. These programs can help you learn more about yourself and help you become a well-rounded person in general. Lastly, participating in such programs is not a condemnation of you or any person. It's a natural and healthy approach to take.

In the next part of this book, you will learn about the techniques and practical strategies you can use to fight the negative effects of anger on a day-to-day basis, for ultimately a more productive and harmonious life.

# PART 2

# TECHNIQUES AND PRACTICAL STRATEGIES TO COMBAT ANGER MANAGEMENT IN THE REAL WORLD

# CHAPTER 6

# AN OPPORTUNITY FOR GROWTH & PERSONAL DEVELOPMENT

Most people tend to not react kindly when they hear the term anger management, especially if it pertains to them. This is because the mere suggestion of undergoing such methods is virtually implying that something is wrong with them. Such negative stigma is not just attached to anger management, but also to other therapeutic methods that are psychological in nature.

For us psychologists, it is not a new phenomena that people don't take it well when suggested that they're in need of anger management. As I have previously stated, his method is not "bad" per se, and when it is advised as a treatment, it's certainly not intended to degrade the person.

Anger management is designed to help people rather than stigmatize them. Therefore such programs are developed to help participants have better control of their anger, such that it does not cause harmful effects to themselves or others. Beyond providing the much needed help in managing anger, these programs can serve as opportunities for personal growth and development.

Here are just some of the ways the right anger management approach can help a person grow and reach their full potential.

## 1. Recognize the things that make you angry

As mentioned earlier, anger episodes just do not come out of nowhere. Almost always, there is something that causes the outburst. Recognizing the things that make you angry is an important component of anger management training.

When you know the things that are making you unhappy and in turn angry, you can make the necessary adjustments that will help you cultivate an appropriate response. Once you identify them, you can work towards fixing them, which will ultimately reduce the incidences of your outbursts. Recognition of what makes you angry is the first, and arguably the most important step in anger management.

## 2. Deal with unhealthy emotions associated with anger

There are multiple emotions associated with anger. They include, but not limited to, aggression and impulsiveness. These associated emotions can cause the potential damage of such episodes to further increase. During anger management sessions, it is not just the anger itself that gets fixed, but also the emotions tied to it.

When you take care of the emotions associated with your anger, you further improve your chances of keeping your rage under control and reduce the potential damage it can cause should you eventually lose control.

## 3. Learn skills for managing triggers

One of the important parts of anger management training is to learn how to manage your triggers. Each person has different triggers I.e. specific factors that cause them to get angry. Part of learning how to manage your anger is learning how to react during those events that typically would make you angry.

This is a multi-step process that modifies your usual response to stressful situations from the ground up. Fixing how you think and react to the things that make you angry is highly beneficial in keeping your anger episodes under control.

I describe this process more thoroughly within "*NLP: A Psychologist's Guide*" but it is equally relevant for a discussion on anger management, so I will include an excerpt from that book below. It is from a chapter titled "Loops Breaks & Pattern Interrupts."

"The brain is undoubtedly an extremely complex organ within the human body. It is required to perform an incredible number of calculations every second even during mundane tasks like guiding the various parts of the body for movement in simple motor skills all the way to making crucial and complex decisions in real time. The brain undertakes millions of these interconnected decisions every single day thereby making it one of the most powerful pieces of biological machinery we have.

However we still do not fully understand the extent of it's complexity and inner workings. One thing we do know is that the brain is solely responsible for enabling people to develop thought patterns and habits that ultimately dictate not only their daily behaviors but also their thinking patterns. It does this in an attempt to optimize a person's day-to-day movements and thought processes, but these short cuts aren't always beneficial.

In order to form these "loops" or "patterns" the brain undertakes several processes that help it both develop a certain habit and make it a part of routine life. In this segment, we will start by taking a brief look at the meaning of cognition in general, which is fairly critical when it comes to NLP. Cognition is simply the study of how the brain perceives information and represents it within the persons mind. It tells us how the brain functions and helps in putting that information to use.

The branch of study that deals with establishing a relationship between learning and cognition is known as neuropsychology, an area of study I once specialized in myself. Neurology has intrigued scientists for as long as the concept has been around with many psychologists having studied its intricacies for decades now. Right from classical conditioning described by Pavlov and John Watson to the operant conditioning of B F Skinner, each one presented theories that described how the human brain works and learns.

It is no secret that a person's daily habits and thinking routines will ultimately dictate how productive and successful they are.

However habits are impartial, they will either help a person attain their desired results and remain persistent in pursuing them. Or they will ensure they continue getting the average/poor results they have always gotten. As Dr Bandler pointed out "Brains aren't designed to get results; they just go in directions".

In terms of general behavior it is usually just a case of learning your ABC's so to speak i.e. learning the sequence of the Antecedent, Behavior and Consequence. This concept was originally based on Skinner's model of cognition, antecedent, behavior and consequence being the three main steps involved in developing a habit. In a nutshell they are described as follows:

## Antecedents

Antecedents are stimuli that precede a behavior or reaction. They are situations and circumstances that cause a person to behave in a certain manner. Antecedents determine the outcome of a certain behavior by inducing it automatically.

In simpler terms, antecedents are people and situations that solicit a certain reaction or behavior. They are what lay down the basis for habits, they hold the key to how a person reacts to any given situation.

Antecedents are studied to know whether the reaction is a result of positive reinforcement or punishment by and large. Having this knowledge makes it easier to predict future behavior. It is fairly simple to manipulate antecedents in order to evoke the desired behavior.

## Behavior

The second component within the habit development model is behavior. Behavior is the response provided to the stimulus. It is meant to serve two main purposes namely to get something that a person desires or to avoid getting something they do not. It is important to note that almost all behavior is learned from significant others. Some is reactionary but all is observable and measurable.

This means that behavior is both visible to others and is a reflection of the person's mind. For example, if a person is angry then their behavior will come through in the form of a changed facial expression or an angry physical reaction. This behavior differs from person to person and is not constant, but rather based on their learned behavior through observing others during past experiences.

As I mention, behavior is also measurable. This means that it is possible for another person to describe the behavior after observation. For example, a person can observe another person getting angry and describe his reaction. This behavior can be altered to give away a desirable outcome.

## Consequence

Consequence is the final component and is a result of the behavior phase. It can be viewed as the environment's reaction to a certain behavior. A consequence will be a direct result of the behavioral action. For example, if a person reacts to a certain situation in a negative manner then the consequence is bound to be negative. Say a person slams a vase on the floor out of anger then it is obvious that the vase will break and the person will have to clean it up. Consequence is also measurable just like behavior.

Basically if you are fully aware of the process I described above you can alter it for your own benefit. It involves understanding the cues, following a routine and availing the consequence/reward. The key here is to aim for the desired results but change the antecedent and rewards, then the behavior will automatically change accordingly.

For example, if you are trying to learn a new skill, but buying books in order to achieve this is not inspiring you enough to study the material then changing over to online classes may inspire you to better effect.

Similarly, you can also change the reward in order to modify the behavior. For example, when trying to excel in a competitive exam, you can look forward to treating yourself to a toy/clothes you have wanted to buy for a long time. Both can work as a motivating factor for you to modify the behavior enough.

The above method works great for changing more general behavioral patterns I find. However we are more concerned with the thinking habits here as opposed to just the behavioral, although they somewhat go hand in hand. That is what real NLP seeks to accomplish. For that you need to view things in a slightly different way, to adopt another approach.

## TOTE Process

With regards to the thinking process in NLP there is a similar structure that the mind follows. It's sometimes described as the path of least resistance approach and is made up of four components the Trigger, Operation, Test and Exit. I'll elaborate on each in a little more detail below:

### Trigger

Similar to the ABC sequence of behavior learning I described above, the TOTE process starts with an antecedent or cue known here as the trigger. In NLP it's also called the 'Anchor' from time to time and once again relates to the impetus or stimulus which starts off the pattern.

### Operation

The operation once again like the ABC process, relates to the behavior portion of the pattern and the thinking habit that we undertake.

**Test**

However this time the mind performs a 'test' of that preceding behavior to identify whether the intended outcome was met or not. Did the person get the desired result from that action? If the answer is 'no', then the person will continue through with the behavior cycle until they do.

**Exit**

If the answer was 'yes' to the test stage, then a person will simply move on with their behavior and proceed to close this thinking pattern loop so to speak. This completion stage must happen in order to not continually go round in circles.

This is how we typically form habits in thinking which can be very powerful cycles especially if built and reinforced over a long period of time. It isn't necessarily a bad thing if this thinking loop is genuinely a beneficial one, but if it is not then it can be quite destructive. We can see this quite clearly in individuals with high obsessive compulsive tendencies (OCD).

In any case these cycles can be reasonably difficult to break but it's imperative that you do so in order to move on from a negative cycle. That is one of the main tenants of NLP, breaking these negative thought patterns to replace with better and more beneficial ones. This process certainly played a critical role to my overall success. When I really learnt how to pattern interrupt.

## Thought Pattern Interrupts

The idea here is to disrupt a negative thought pattern as early on in the cycle/sequence as possible, more specifically between the trigger and the operation. Regardless it must be completed before the testing phase of the condition, to say that you must disrupt it before the mind tries to test the original operation pattern otherwise any attempt to break the sequence will be of little use as the pattern is almost completed.

The pattern interrupts aren't that difficult to implement and it is simply about stopping your train of thought and thinking about something different, butting in on your own thought process/ conversation you are having within your own head.

Like Richard Bandler suggests, we are simply trying to change the direction of the mind and reprogram it as we do. You are not removing the old pattern per se, but rather redirecting around it.

**Go big!**

The idea is to make this interrupt as big and bold as possible. If there is one mistake I see from people who try this method is that they are too weak with their disrupting action and it isn't enough to fully divert their thinking. Especially if it is a long term entrenched habit of thought they are trying to break.

Try a loud clap of the hands or loud cough. If the cycle which is trying to be broken is a negative thought process with depressive emotions attached to it, then try breaking the pattern with a little dance/jig or a laugh. Try to inject humor into the disrupt as it is completely counter to the original and unwanted behavior and congruent with the newer, happier thought process.

**Timing is Everything**

As I described above, timing is everything here. You need to ensure you catch the trigger phase as accurately as you can as it will be key to identifying when you need to employ the pattern disrupt. In essence this should be directly after and as soon as possible following on from when the trigger is spotted.

However in reality this is likely to be a very short period of time so you really have to be a keen observant throughout the day to catch them when they do occur. For me it was usually some thought or memory which popped into my head that would start the cycle, especially the negative ones.

If I let it continue, my emotions and physiology would start to change when in it would be too late. I have now learnt to catch this right before this transition takes place i.e right after the trigger thought/memory and replace my momentary operation/behavior to a more positive one.

**Rinse & Repeat**

However that is simply not enough in my experience, just catching the cycle once. The real payoff comes from repeating this cycle over and over until the new behavior pattern becomes habitual and you start to see the results you are looking for.

So make sure you perform whatever interrupt you have chosen until it becomes second nature to you, until you no longer have to think about it. You have to bring the skill into the "Unconscious Competence" phase when performing it. That is when the new direction of thought and subsequent behavior will really take hold.

This general approach was taken from hypnotherapists such as Milton Erickson who used pattern interrupts to disrupt the waking thinking patterns of their participants. They would lead a persons inner monologue down a familiar path before disrupting the line of questioning leaving the persons unconscious mind waiting for the logical next step of the pattern to occur, but it never comes. This can be a powerful enough confusion of the mind which puts a certain percentage of the population into a hypnotic trance.

You are not attempting to go that far with yourself and it's almost impossible to do it on your own, but the general thought pattern interrupt is designed to work along the same lines. But this time to disrupt a familiar negative thought pattern such as anger and replace with a more positive and beneficial one."

## 4. Learn how to stay calm

It is never easy to keep yourself calm, especially when you are subjected to a stressful situation. However similar to the thought pattern interrupt process described previously, the good news is that it is a skill that can be learned and mastered. Even the most hot-headed of people can learn how to control their emotions and transform them into healthier responses. There are different techniques that can help you become calmer in the face of situations that can make you angry.

There are mindfulness exercises that teach you how to control your emotions. There are relaxation techniques that help you in keeping calm during specific scenarios. Learning to stay calm is one of the most important skills you will acquire in anger management (more on this later).

## 5. Become a better problem solver

An inability to manage or solve specific issues is linked to the development of anger and frustration. As such, it is also an important component of anger management programs to teach people how to solve such problems. Knowing how to manage issues the right way is empowering, and can greatly reduce any feelings of frustration that a person might feel.

Becoming a better manager of problems is a multi-step process. Knowing how to see the problem properly, assessing the right way to approach issues, and looking for the best solutions are just some of the skills you can master to become a better problem solver in life.

When you try to look at things more closely, you will see that the effects of anger management problems go beyond just controlling anger. It can help you become a better person overall. Taking on a program such as this just might help unlock your potential that you never thought you had.

The following chapters of this book will talk about the various parts of anger management programs. You may need some of the elements here more than others depending on your personal situation, but each part is valuable in their own unique ways. That's just the way it is with anger management: a holistic approach that seeks to rebuild the person in a 360 fashion will always reap the best results.

# CHAPTER 7

# ALTERING THE EMOTIONAL BALANCE - SHIFTING PERCEPTIONS

"Forgive others not because they deserve forgiveness, but because you deserve peace"

(Jonathon Lockwood Huie)

Psychologists will often state that the way in which a person view things will have a huge say on how they are bound to live their life. By modifying your perception so to speak, you become capable of changing a lot of things in your life, including the way you express your anger.

One of the most vital components of anger management is learning how to shift the emotional balance. Changing your perceptions goes a long way in controlling your anger and being able to harness it in a healthier manner later down the line. When you change your perception, your actions and reactions will also change with it.

Any kind of behavior is seen to have a perspective component. How you see yourself, others, and the world has a drastic effect on your behavior. It basically dictates how you would act based on both internal and external stimuli. While you cannot have full control on the perception of others, you do have full control over your own perception.

Take this for example: Supposing you are in a room with a number of other people. You might think that the temperature is cold, while others may think it's hot. The takeaway here is that how you interpret things may not be the same as how others interpret it.

How powerful exactly is perception in determining our emotions though? Think of it this way: your perception of the world and the things that happen in it affects your attitude. If intense rage and emotions blind your perspective, it shall consume you and every action that you will make.

Your actions will be dictated by your desire to get even, to prove that you're better than everyone else, and to prove others wrong, just to name a few. You would view other people as targets; people are "just the same" and are all out to get you perhaps. Your perceptions can get tainted by anger, and the results are not exactly going to be pretty.

Related to this, your perception of what's happening in your life also alters your emotional state. When you are happy, you tend to view things in a more positive light, even when some things are not exactly going your way. You always see the bright side of things, and therefore you can keep things in better perspective.

On the flipside, when you are not happy, your view of things and situations is negative – bad, wrong, a mistake, heartbreaking, a challenge, etc. You tend to believe that every aspect of your life isn't turning out how you would like it to.

So, you start to focus on the things you don't like or have, and that will further amplify your feelings of frustration. This would then manifest into anger bursts or put you in a constant state of frustration.

It's somewhat of a 'chicken or egg' scenario. Which one comes first? An event which in turn either makes us happy or sad depending on our perception of it? Or our perception of the event either making it good or bad for us? The event is neutral and exactly the same either way. The trick though is to be on the causal side I.e. get out ahead of the event with a positive perception of it to begin with. Don't leave yourself open to a negative reaction just because you perceive situations in a negative light in general.

While we cannot affect the perception of others, we are still influenced by them nonetheless. As humans, we are always concerned with how other people see us. We do not want to be perceived as foolish, so we adjust and/or alter our behaviors to fit in.

While there are scenarios wherein such a conformist attitude is good and beneficial, there are situations that this is considered as a maladaptive practice. It puts an unnecessary burden on ourselves, and chances are they are not going to change their perspectives of you and your actions anyway. This can cause feelings of frustration, and may eventually lead to a buildup of negative emotions such as anger.

To sum everything up, it is crucial for you to shift your perceptions to take control of your internal emotional state and anger issues as a result. You cannot modify the things that are happening to you, but you can certainly modify how you are going to react to them. If something makes you angry, modifying the way you react to such a situation will help you avoid an outburst.

Making a conscious effort in avoiding triggers and changing your response to irritating stimuli will help you overcome your anger management issues. Aside from self-help techniques, you can also use treatments such as cognitive behavioral therapy to resolve your perceptional issues.

# CHAPTER 8

# KNOWING WHAT DRIVES YOUR ANGER

"Anger is never without a reason, but seldom with a good one"

(Benjamin Franklin)

Just to recap what we have already discussed, anger is a secondhand emotion. Its never a problem in isolation, but rather a result of some underlying issue that just gets triggered into life by some momentary event. Knowing what this dissonance causing factor is, is a critical component of anger management. It shines a light on the true nature of the problem, thus giving you an idea of how you can deal with it and subsequently limit your anger episodes.

What drives your anger? This chapter will guide you in identifying the factors that could be triggering things for you and then teach you some techniques on how to potentially eliminate them.

There are a lot of situations wherein a random event spontaneously triggers anger. However, it is more common that an angry reaction was derived from something that has always been there under the surface as we've already seen.

I am talking about triggers, internal or external factors that elicit anger from you. Most people think that the thing which has made them angry is the person or the situation, but the real reason behind their anger is a preconditioned sensitivity to certain stimuli. For different reasons, specific scenarios or circumstances make you angry.

How do these triggers develop? Some may think that anger triggers are hereditary, but while one's propensity for getting hot-headed may be linked to genetic factors in part, the majority of these characteristics are indeed acquired naturally, they are learned from our environment and society in general. A combination of norms, personal experience, and cultivated values help in forming your triggers and shape your level of sensitivity towards them.

For example, those who were victims of bullying are triggered by acts of real or perceived bullying. Also, victims of war or a terrorist attack tend to have a prejudice to groups of people thought to be associated with the perpetrators. Another example would be people trained in military-style households who get mad at undisciplined behavior.

Starting as early as our formative years, these triggers gradually develop over time. In fact, while these triggers can be developed virtually anywhere, they are mostly built right in our own homes. The values your family instilled in you, the relationships you share with your folks, and even the type of media content you are exposed to while at home all play a factor in forming your triggers.

Of course, just because the triggers of your anger may lie deep within, it doesn't mean that you cannot do something to combat them. You can manage your anger by identifying the things that cause your anger and changing the way you react to them. Of course, the first step down this road is the process of identifying what makes you angry.

Among the common triggers for anger include being treated unfairly, feelings of frustration and disappointment, being pressured, experiencing failure, encountering threats to your self-esteem, being attacked emotional or physically, and being wronged by other people in general.

Ask yourself this question: what are the things that drive you mad? Why does it make you mad? What do you usually do when you get mad? From there, you can create a plan of action to resolve it.

Now that you have identified the things that make you angry, it is now time to do something about your anger triggers. It must be mentioned that resolving your triggers does not happen overnight. The good news is that this has been done before.

When you follow the process in the right way, you can actually resolve your triggers eventually. We have touched on some of the aspects earlier on but here is how you take care of your anger triggers once you have identified them.

## 1. Take responsibility

The first step in working on your triggers is to take responsibility for it. If something makes you angry, no matter how seemingly minor or embarrassing it may be, you should hold yourself accountable for it. No matter what the circumstances, you still played a role in the development of such a situation. Once you recognize that you have a problem, that is only the time that you will finally be able to begin the healing process.

## 2. Avoid blaming

It is common for people to blame others for their problems with anger. After all, the common reasoning when one becomes angry is to say, "this or that caused me to become angry". You must constantly remind yourself that no matter what happened, it is still you who chose to become angry. Blaming it on others would only compound your problems and defer the responsibility away from yourself as it would make it seem that you're justifying your acts.

## 3. Reflect on it

Once everything has sunk in for you, reflect on the things that make you angry all of the time. How did it all begin? Why does it trigger you the way that it does? Is there a justifiable reason to keep doing it this way? Is it possible for you to do things differently?

Reflect on all of these points, as it will help you see what your problems really are and what kind of solutions you need. You can do this reflection by yourself, or you can do it within a supportive peer group.

## 4. Just fix it

It is not enough that you now know what your problem is. Now that you know what the root cause of your frustration is, it is important that you have the resolve to do whatever it takes to fix it. Acknowledging is different from acting on it.

Once you have identified your problem points and triggers, it is important that you make the necessary steps resolve them. The road to getting it done is not going to be easy, but there is no reason that you cannot make it.

My advice would be to go back to the previous chapter and run through the 'Thought Pattern Interrupt" process with every major issue and trigger point you have. Start on the road to fixing the behavioral responses you have to them, I promise you it will be a worthwhile exercise in regards to leading a more peaceful, anger free life.

# CHAPTER 9

# DEALING WITH ANGER - DEFUSING THE TICKING TIME BOMB

"People who fly into rage, always make a bad landing"

(Will Rogers)

Despite your best efforts in dealing with the triggers that cause anger outbursts and your subsequent behavior patterns to such instances, there are still other, more holistic approaches you can take to make sure you have all bases covered.

You can never fully control what you will encounter in your day-to-day experience, but you can always control how you will respond to it. Anger may be like a ticking time bomb inside of us, but we can always defuse it by using the right techniques.

There is always a way to appropriately deal with anger. This chapter will explore a couple of techniques that I have personally used in dealing with anger throughout certain periods in my life so you may also use them to defuse and avoid the potentially destructive effects of anger yourself.

## 1. Relaxation Techniques

When you are dealing with anger, taking a step back to relax can be extremely beneficial. Relaxation techniques, aside from helping bursts of anger subside, are a great way to relieve stress and anxiety. It also contributes to creating a general feeling of wellness in the first place.

There are many relaxation techniques available for you. It's just about learning how to keep your stress level balanced and within tolerable levels. Never miss the opportunity to relax whenever necessary. It will also help if you keep your worries to a minimum, as too much pointless postulation always leads to unnecessary stress.

Breathing techniques, exercise, laughter therapy, and other techniques can also help you in letting off steam. Make it a habit to stay relaxed. Your body and mind will thank you for it.

## 2. Mindfulness

Along the same lines, mindfulness is defined as the awareness of the present, both in terms of moment and circumstance. Deriving its roots from Buddhism, this concept has since gained all kinds of applications, both in the field of psychology and beyond. It is effective in both managing anger and preventing outbursts from happening, as it helps in calming down the mind and leaving problems behind.

How can you practice mindfulness? Firstly, you have to pay attention to everything that's happening around you, all the sights, sounds, distractions. Everything. Secondly, you have to try and focus on just one element of your existing moment like your breath to help you fall into a peaceful mediation. But most importantly of all, ensuring that you keep all of your focus on the present moment.

Mindfulness is not easy to master, but once you do so, it is a powerful tool. If you find it too tricky at first, you can ask the help of an expert to guide you in your mindfulness training. There are many excellent books on the topic that delve into it's practices and benefits in much more detail than I can here. So my advice is to do your research and start down the road on your mindful journey yourself. My personal favorite is *"The Power of Now"* by Eckhart Tolle. It was a game changer for me.

But in general, defusing the ticking time bomb inside you is difficult. However, if there's one person who can do it, it has to be you. Use the techniques mentioned here, as well as other techniques you find effective, to prevent anger from taking over.

# CHAPTER 10

# CONFLICT RESOLUTION TECHNIQUES

"Peace is not the absence of conflict but the presence of creative alternatives for responding to conflict. Alternatives to passive or aggressive responses. Alternatives to violence"

(Dorothy Thompson)

Everyone faces conflicts from time to time, they are often what set off angry reactions within ourselves. In fact, you will run into some form of conflict most days to varying degrees, whether this is within yourself or regarding the people around you. Your ability to resolve these conflicts will help make your life easier and much more stress-free.

On the flipside, the inability to manage conflicts leads to frustration and stress, which can later snowball into anger and even rage. As such, developing conflict resolution skills is considered an important part of anger management. Aside from improving your skills in managing inner and outer conflicts, improving conflict resolution skills can be highly empowering.

Why is it considered important to develop conflict resolution or problem solving skills? The first reason is obvious: we are facing problems on a day-to-day basis. Failing to recognize or deal with these problems appropriately can worsen the situation further.

The second reason is that it gives us a systematic approach to facing our problems. A systematic approach works in both the macro and micro settings, helping you manage the bigger aspects of your life, and down to its smallest details.

Resolving conflicts is accomplished by way of a systematic approach for the most optimal results. Regardless of the type of issue you are having, such an approach can help you fix your problems in the most efficient way possible.

Here is a brief look at the process of how you can go about solving some of your conflicting problems:

## 1. Identify the problem

To solve a problem, you firstly need to recognize that a problem exists. Establish what the problem is. It is imperative that you are specific with the goals that you want to accomplish, whilst you are also aiming to resolve the conflict at hand. It is possible to have a primary goal, with it being subdivided into smaller ones.

At the same time, you also need to identify the barriers that could either prevent you from resolving your problem or make it more difficult or complicated than it should be. You must recognize any potential barrier to achieving your goal and find ways on how you can get around them.

## 2. Get a better picture of the problem

Knowing that you have a problem is the first step in the conflict resolution process. The next step is to know more about the issue at hand. Get as much information as you can about the conflict, getting as many perspectives as possible.

You also need to search for facts relevant to your problem, as failing to gather enough evidence or even the wrong information can only compound your problems in the long run. Get the facts straight and do not rely on just what your intuition is saying. It only takes a few moments to see the full picture in simple conflicts, but you might need to think long and hard on more complicated situations.

## 3. Find solutions

Now that you have analyzed the conflict, it is now time to find the appropriate solutions to your problem. Whether you are taking this problem on individually or as part of the group, brainstorming is important. Come up with all possible solutions. If other people are involved, let their sides be heard, and then make sure to come up with a collaborative decision. Once you have analyzed all options, it is time for you to make a choice.

Find the best solution to your problem based on the details of the conflict, potential obstacles, available resources, and expertise at hand. Of course, keep alternatives on standby just in case you need a change of approach in the event that your current methods aren't providing the changes you need to see.

**4. Put things into action**

After all the planning and decision making, it is time to put things into action. It is important that you put your solutions into play, otherwise nothing is going to happen.

During implementation, you might discover other problems that would also need your attention. You can create a plan on how you can resolve the additional problems, modify your plan to take account of what you encountered, or change course altogether if deemed appropriate. The important thing here is during implementation, you always need to be prepared and expect the unexpected.

After implementation, do a proper evaluation to see if your plan worked accordingly, and if you can further improve on it later down the line.

Learning basic conflict management skills is one of the keys to a successful life in general. It can go a long way in keeping your frustrations to a minimum. Aside from providing an answer to most of your problems, proper conflict management will provide that much needed self-esteem boost. It even teaches you how to become more assertive, giving you greater control of your day-to-day circumstance. Use conflict management to your advantage and keep those anger triggers at bay.

One of the most beneficial exercises I used to perform whilst building my business in the early years (and still do to some degree) is "Resolving Conflicting Parts" within myself. I have included a bonus chapter on how to do this at the end of this book. The process I describe is geared towards other psychological conflicts I had at the time but it can absolutely be applied to parts within a person that make them fearful, frustrated and angry. So make sure you give it a good try.

# CHAPTER 11

# BREAKING THE CYCLE OF FRUSTRATING AND PROBLEMATIC RELATIONSHIPS

"If another can easily anger you, it is because you are off balance with yourself"

(Scottie Waves)

One of the most common reasons people feel a sense of anger is because of failed relationships. Just about everyone has experienced failure in relationships at one point or another in their lives. Some failures hurt more than others, and therefore have a bigger potential to alter a person's attitude and perspective.

One of the ways to reduce the anger you feel inside is to both resolve and prevent frustrating and problematic relationships. Essentially, if you want a happy life, you will need to break this cycle.

Here is the step-by-step process on how you can do just that:

## 1. Assess your attitude

There are a lot of times when the cause of your problematic relationships is actually you, yourself. It is either you choose to stick with toxic relationships or you are the one who is making it toxic but cannot see it.

So initially you need to assess if you are the problem. There are times when it's your resolve to stay in a frustrating relationship. There are people with compromised standards, who have the desire to seek superficial relationships, and stick to those who test their morals and standards.

There are also times when the person has attitude problems which in turn causes people to get turned off with them. Assess your own attitude before you look at others. You'll never know when the cause of your problems just might be you.

## 2. Be kind

Kindness is one of the most valuable ingredients in building great relationships. People naturally gravitate towards people who are kind.

I mean, who doesn't like to interact with someone who will warmly welcome you? Also, when you treat people kindly, they tend to treat you in the same fashion. It's the law of reciprocity at work.

Additionally, being kind gives off a positive vibe to your everyday life, leaving less space for anger and bitterness to enter. No matter how people treat you, do not be afraid to show kindness every day.

Start with making a habit to smile more, it will cost you nothing but have a monumental payoff on your interactions with others. Just be thankful and appreciative what you have, including the presence of other people in your life. Take the time to help and complement others also. Those are just some of the simple ways you can express kindness, so compound as many as you can. More the better here.

## 3. Break the desire to get even

When you are caught in the cycle of bad relationships, it is easy to fall into a trap of desiring to get even. When you feel that you have been wronged, more likely than not, you will be looking for revenge. It doesn't have to be that way, that you have to retaliate against those who have spited you. The desire to get even will be reflected in the way we treat others, it's wasted energy taking away from your progress and overall happiness in life.

As such, if you want to maintain meaningful relationships, you will need to break the desire to get even. Learn to forgive others while also learning to forgive yourself. Accept the fact that you've been hurting and look for ways to resolve it, and then move on.

## 4. Choose relationships wisely

Breaking the cycle of bad relationships means making the effort to pick the right relationships in the first place. It doesn't matter that you had good intentions. If you keep getting into bad relationships, it is more likely than not going to end badly.

It may seem strange, but a lot of people get into the habit of entering into bad relationships subconsciously. From caring for people who don't care for them to getting attached with people who constantly gives you trust issues, a lot of people keep looking for love in all the wrong places.

If you want to break the cycle of frustrating relationships, make it a point to choose your relationships wisely for the outset. This can be easier said then done but not doing so will only set you up for more heartache in the future.

## 5. Both sides should make things work

Relationships on all levels are a two-way street. For them to thrive, both sides should make the effort in making things work. Now, there are multiple ways for both sides to find a middle ground that will benefit everyone.

Firstly, communication lines should remain open all the time. You should learn to speak out, but you should always listen to what the other side is saying. Both sides should make it a point to build mutual trust. You and the other person should make it an effort to make each other better, to create an environment where the "whole is greater than the sum of its parts."

Much of our anger and frustrations are tied to our inability to create and maintain healthy relationships. As such, it is basically a given that if you want to manage your anger, you have got to manage your relationships better. It will not be the ultimate cure for your frustrations and problems, but it will make your life in general so much more peaceful as a result.

# CHAPTER 12

# THE BENEFITS OF ANGER - IT'S NOT ALL BAD

Anger is often viewed as a purely negative emotion. It is considered in this light usually for good reason. It also comes with the accusation of being the cause of just about any bad deed ranging from ill-advised impulsive decisions to criminal behavior. However, anger per se is not the enemy. In fact, it can be a constructive emotion in a wide range of ways if you direct the facets of this type of behavior appropriately.

There are even situations when expressing your anger becomes a necessity. It has been shown throughout history as well as scientific literature that anger can cause positive transformations if directed in the right way. It can be a source of motivation, a means for improving social ties, and a catalyst for change. Anger is not all bad, and there are real benefits that can be had from it. Again, if you know how to manage it.

What has been the reason for anger as an emotion gaining such a bad reputation? Firstly, it could be due to the fact that anger is often associated with violence and inappropriate behavior. During angry episodes, the risk of losing control, acting inappropriately, and behaving indifferently is higher indeed.

In addition, society frowns upon the emotion of rage, especially if it is projected the wrong way. While there are people who know how to keep their rage under control, not everyone can do that with flying colors. Sometimes, it's due to the situation or circumstances a person finds themselves in. But as I've mentioned many times, its usually due to some underlying issue or predisposition to anger.

All of these factors play a role in the bad reputation that anger has. Anger is a much maligned emotion for good reason for the most part. However, many people miss the fact that it's an emotion that can be beneficial as well. As I also mentioned earlier, anger is a primal adaptation that helped humans survive throughout history.

There are different ways in which it has proven to be advantageous over the ages. What are these specific benefits though? Here is a list of some of them:

## 1. Relationship Building

As strange as it may initially sound, and as counter this may seem in relation to the previous chapter, anger can have a beneficial effects within relationships on occasions. As much as it is attributed to the deterioration of bonds between people and a breaking of rapport, a little bit of rage can serve as a galvanizing force (if it is harnessed properly).

Anger can serve as a stimulus for people to see that something is wrong. They can use this energy to initiate a resolution to their problems.

Anger can also serve as a much needed wake-up call when relationships go south. When expressed properly and not resorting to hurtful stuff, anger can greatly help in building relationships in the long run if managed well in small bursts.

## 2. A Source of Motivation

Historically, anger has always served as one of the most potent motivational sources out there. When people experience bitter setbacks in life, the most productive way to make up for it is to use the pain they felt as motivation to continue learning and be better the next time around. Anger can serve as the much needed extra push that will help take you to the next level.

If you don't let your rage consume you negatively, the anger you feel may serve you well. Instead of letting your rage consume you, channel it into power. Utilize this powerful emotion to unlock your full potential.

## 3. A Catalyst for Needed Change

Throughout history, we have seen how anger can help change history. While this emotion is almost exclusively attributed to starting wars and a lot of senseless bloodshed, anger has also led to much needed reforms and cultural transformation. When you look at it, anger may prove to be that critical ingredient for us to keep moving forward.

Let your anger push you to challenge injustices around you. Allow it to motivate you in pursuing higher goals and causes. Let your anger help you defend yourself, others, and the things you believe in. When you express it the right way, your rage can be the catalyst for needed change.

## 4. Strategic Purposes

Along the same lines as the above two points, anger can provide you with a strategic advantage if you know how to harness it to your benefit. Expressing your anger is a great way to show that you are not backing down from a challenge and that anybody can just walk all over you.

Use your anger to influence the kind of change that you want. You can also use anger to get other people in line. Often used as a last resort, showing that you're angry will send the message across, and would usually lead to the eventual correction of the issues at hand. When expressed within a constructive framework, your anger will help you accomplish what you need to to.

Much has been said about expressing your anger in a healthy manner. But the big question is this; how can you do it? Your anger should first be rationalized. There should be a method to the madness, so to speak. This comes with practice.

You can't be mad just because you wanted to be mad; you just need to channel the natural anger which comes to the surface. Secondly, you should try to weigh in the positive and negative effects of letting this emotion take over you. Never let anger give you a false sense of entitlement or a justification to do things that are overtly wrong.

Thirdly, your expression of rage should always remain controlled. This is where your maturity comes into play. Express your frustrations, let it lift you up, but do not let it dominate you and push you into making careless mistakes.

# SUMMARY

My early academic life was concerned primarily with studying the intricacies of every branch of neuropsychology available. It gave me a great understanding on how the brain functions on an anatomical level, but as I mentioned within the open remarks to this book, it wasn't until I made my way in the "real world" did I start to really piece the psychological puzzle together.

Some of these area's include more psychotherapeutic disciplines like cognitive behavioral therapy along with anger management. How to deal with manipulation in your life as well as increasing your overall emotional intelligence. They all fit together to ultimately give you that peace of mind you are looking for.

With regards to anger management specifically, it's beneficial to start at the beginning. To see exactly what the causes of you anger are in the first place. What are the underlying factors in your life which are making you unhappy to begin with? If you can identify these irritation points within yourself, you have a much higher chance of eradicating anger issues naturally.

However there are some common triggers to look out for in addition to your underlying issues. Only you know what these are, and it's up to you to deal with them when they do arise. I have included the description on how the "Thought Pattern Interrupt" process works for dealing with negative triggers on a day-to-day basis. It would be greatly beneficial to go through this process with anything you know sends you into a negative tailspin.

It's also about taking responsibility for your thoughts and feelings and dealing with them as such. I've lost count of the times someone has done something stupid in my businesses or life in general. It used to make me extremely frustrated, however these days I know it's up to me how I react to these instances. I know it was me who chose to get angry with the person or situation. However that rarely changes anything for the better.

Saying that, a little bit of anger pointed in the right direction can push you forward if you control it correctly. If you mange to utilize this energy to further a business or fitness endeavor you are working towards. Or spark your stagnating relationship back into life.

However you need to be careful here and never let it turn into rage, that is never constructive as all bets are off. But you might find letting off just a little steam in the right instances does the job. That is presuming you are in the right type of relationship to begin with of course.

Lastly, you want to make sure you are taking a holistic approach to your anger management. You must ensure that not only are you looking at your issues from a problem solving, cognitive standpoint, but also from a lifestyle perspective. I could only touch on these concepts within this book but the benefits of starting down the road of relaxation, mindfulness and meditation cannot be overstated enough.

There are many great books and teachers on these subjects so go hunt them down and give them a try. I know for me it was one of, if not the most significant contributor to my success, relationships and overall well-being.

# CONCLUSION

"Workout your own salvation. Do not depend on others"

(Buddha)

I started off this book with a quote from the Buddha himself and I would like to finish with one also. I know that the path to fixing anger management issues is not an easy one, no psychological journey ever is. But that isn't to say you should not start down the road of improvement, it will be so worth it in the long run. But it's you who needs to take the first step.

I'm not saying you shouldn't seek help and guidance along the way, you certainly should. But ultimately it starts and ends with you. No matter how bad you perceive your current situation or upbringing to be, you are the only one who can change it. You are the one who has the power to change how you think about it.

As I have mentioned previously, it's all about perception here. "Change the way you look at things and the things you look at change" is one of the truest things I've ever heard. So make sure you are taking a hard and honest look at your life. Look at where you are and where you would like to be. The root cause of your anger will almost certainly be a result of some dissonance between the two.

It's now up to you to go and find out what these factors are. Hopefully I have given you some pointers and observations on how to do just that, how to deal with anger management issues within your life a little better. So go ahead and put some of these strategies into place today!

I wish you the very best of luck.

# BONUS CHAPTERS

(From 'Emotional Intelligence: A Psychologist's Guide')

# CHAPTER 4

# TAKING INVENTORY OF YOUR EMOTIONAL STATE

"Educating the mind without educating the heart is no education
at all"

(Aristotle)

One of the most important things you can do when initially
starting out on your emotional intelligence enhancing journey is
to take stock of what you are currently feeling. There is no right
or wrong answers here in terms of what come up. As our limbic
legacy show us, humans are inherently emotional creatures and
suppressing them is almost impossible to do entirely.

However you do have control over the way you react to these
tendencies, the thoughts and behaviors after the fact. The following
factors should help you take a closer look into how to identify and
deal with these feelings when they do arise to ultimately move you
to the next level in your E.Q. journey.

## Acknowledge Your Emotions

The first thing to do when attempting to increase your personal E.Q. levels is to get good at acknowledging and perceiving the emotions that you are feeling. This is the starting point for every model and framework of E.Q.

Whenever I feel an emotion arise within me I always take a pause and acknowledge its presence, I take a moment and really feel it so I can understand and label it in my mind. This isn't the same as reacting or acting upon the emotion just yet, but I want to know why it may have arisen and if it could be useful to me. If it's a feeling of anger, fear or frustration I do not deny or try to hide it, but instead acknowledge its presence and dismiss it as not being productive and move on.

If you start to dwell on emotions such as these you will quickly fall into a negative spiral thought process that will have you framing everything in a pessimistic light before you know it. I used to play out entire imaginary scenarios in my head of something going badly and the knock-on effects that I 'knew' it would have, only to realize that it NEVER worked out that badly and that I'd fabricated it all in my mind. Sound familiar?

If on the other hand it is an emotion of excitement, joy or anticipation, I also pause for a moment, acknowledge and label what it is that I'm feeling and try to cultivate and utilize it if I think it will benefit the situation such as situational empathy (which we will get onto later).

It is also important to take responsibility for these emotions that you are feeling either way, good or bad. Know that it is something inside of you which is eliciting such a response and that you have to deal with it and not sweep it under the carpet so to speak. This is usually the most challenging step for people, but it is also the most rewarding. Yes it maybe some outside influence or stimulus that sparked the response in the first place, but remember that the emotions you are feeling are coming from within you and that it's your responsibility to deal with them

## Understand That You Are Not Your Emotions

So following on from that, you also need to constantly remind yourself that the emotions which arise within you and the conscious entity which interprets them are two very different things. Most people walk around in somewhat of a waking sleep for the most part completely at the mercy of any feeling, thought or emotion that pops into their head.

You have to understand that many thoughts and emotions will pass through you almost on a second by second basis, but again it's entirely your choice on how you perceive and choose to react to them.

There is also a very large egoic element to this process as well. Thoughts and feelings of jealously for another person or fear of performing a task is really just your ego trying to keep your preconceived notions about the world intact and keep you operating within your comfort zone. This is a topic for much greater discussion i.e. regarding the tactics to counteract such self-sabotaging behavior, but needless to say that detaching yourself from your overall emotional state is very a beneficial thing to do.

## Learn to Forgive Yourself & Others

"Life becomes easier when you learn to accept an apology you never got"

(Robert Brault)

Again, along the same lines as letting go of a negative emotion that arises within you, people have a great tendency to hold onto what they perceive to be negative acts that they have either committed themselves or others against them. Holding onto this ill feeling again serves absolutely no purpose to you in the immediate future and certainly not the long run. *"Holding onto anger is like drinking poison and expecting the other person to die"* as the Buddha so aptly put it.

If there was one thing that got me ahead in my business life so quickly it was this concept. Once I stopped getting caught up with what I thought I deserved from a situation or others around me and started pushing ahead regardless, I made so much more

ANGER MANAGEMENT

progress. You can't stop and throw stones at every dog that barks, and that includes yourself when you mess up.

This isn't just applicable to adult and business life either, it's relates to everyone young or old. If I had taken heed of this advice when I was growing up I know I would have had better overall relationships with school/college friends and family alike. That's not to say things were necessarily that bad, but they could have been better, or at least I could have saved myself a great deal of heart ache and stress along the way.

**Don't Get Involved in Negative Self-Talk**

As I mentioned above, letting negative self talk get out of hand is a very bad habit to take up. I would say that it is the one thing that plagues humanity more than anything. We often talk ourselves out of things before we've had a chance to start them. Again this comes down to letting negative thoughts and emotions cloud our thinking to a point of almost no escape. You have to stop this in its tracks as quickly as possible if you want to build high overall levels of emotional intelligence.

This also includes negative self-talk and 'gossip' regarding other people. In danger of sounding like one of your parents or school teachers here, you don't need me to tell you this is a worthless exercise and one that will ultimately bring your E.Q. level down with it. No one is perfect; just make a point of catching yourself when you start to talk in this way.

Also along the same lines as the above, you must try and do your best not to judge others where ever possible. This actually freed me greatly in a psychological sense when I managed to stop doing it a few years ago. I never thought of myself as an overly judgmental person but I still realized I would do it from time to time. But stopping myself altogether from judging anyone I came across in even the smallest way saves me so much mental energy and almost certain daily miss judgment.

Nowadays I simply let others go about their day in their own way without even the slightest judging thought about their behavior. That is not to say that I tolerate bad behavior or that I do not try and empathize with people and attempt to understand their situation better, which is critical to building fruitful relationships. But I don't judge them with regards to how they got to where they are, I never walked in their shoes or went through the struggles they did so I let them do the talking on this one.

Again this isn't some "holier than thou" situation, I'm not perfect and do very occasionally catch myself automatically judging someone. I just now catch it very early and stop myself in my tracks straight away. It's so much more liberating when you do.

# BONUS CHAPTER

(From 'NLP: A Psychologist's Guide')

# CHAPTER 5

# RESOLVING CONFLICTING PARTS

"We don't see things as they are; we see them as we are"

(Anais Nin)

So in addition to remonstrating conflicting emotional events by collapsing the anchors which surround them in your mind, a similar technique can be used to rectify differences within your internal thinking 'parts'. That may sound like a strange thing to say, but humans are made up of many voices within our own heads and often times they are very conflicting and it's difficult to know which one to listen to.

Firstly lets identify exactly what I mean here, naturally you will have a professional or office part which usually behaves in a certain way like holding up a great deal of decorum around colleagues. You will also have a family part (often a different one for either parent).

For me personally my mother was rather strict and a perfectionist and I would have to act in a certain way to appease her if I got a bad grade at school for example. I would automatically go into excuse mode around her, it was like a protection mechanism against it. However my father was much more relaxed and I would be able to have more open discussions with him as a result.

You will also have an entrepreneurial part to you that likely kicks you into gear from time to time to try out that new business venture. A similar fitness part may get you to the gym consistently for a period of time. You will also have a self-development part which is likely responsible for you buying this book.

Conversely you will have counter parts to these seemingly positive voices. You will have the fun loving part, the voice in your head which says "you only live once, go out and enjoy things as you will regret it when you are older". Then there is the lazy part which will want you to sit around all day and do nothing. This should be quite an obvious one to silence most of the time. However it can be difficult to resolve the inner conversations of the other parts sometimes, especially as they seemingly all have positive payoffs.

Firstly it is a good idea to get out a pen and paper and begin to note down the dominant parts that you feel influence your life and thinking the most. You must be as honest as possible here as the more accurately you can do this the better outcome you will ultimately achieve for yourself. Essentially you are just having a conversation with yourself here so nobody else has to know.

Note them all down, your perfectionist part, your procrastination part, your creative part, your fear part etc. Then it is about picking the handful which really effect your life the most and that are most conflicted with each other. Separate them out and ask each of them what it is they bring to the table, what are they trying to do for you? Then write these down also.

For me these main conflicting parts in my early adult life were my entrepreneurial business building part and my carefree fun loving part. I kind of felt that I should start building the foundations to my consultancy business when I left college but another side of me just wanted to go backpacking around Europe. For you it might be something similar or some other combination of the above examples.

Then it is about having a parts negotiation session. Again I will use the example of my conflicting parts so you get an idea of what I mean. Much like the collapsing anchors technique in the previous chapter you need to place each conflicting part in the palms of each hand. Again you need to visualize what they both look like. This can be anything but it's important to do as it will be coming from you subconscious mind.

For me the entrepreneurial part looked like a lady in a business suit carrying a leather case filled with important documents much like a lawyer would. The fun loving part was me at around nine years old in an over sized t-shirt and cowboy hat I used to take from my older brother. It is also a beneficial idea to attach any emotions that arise with these visual parts when you bring them up.

Now you want to put yourself in the shoes of one of the parts and really feel what it is thinking, ask it what it is giving you but also what it thinks of the conflicting part opposite it. I would discover that the entrepreneurial part just wanted me to get ahead in life and plan for the future, it would say that it is delaying gratification as the bigger payoff will come later. It disliked the fun loving part as it felt it got in the way of progress and was a waste of time.

I then put myself in the shoes of the fun loving part, I also asked it what it was giving to me. It said that it didn't want me to waste my youth and that I would miss the times going out with my friends to party with them etc and that when I grew up there would be plenty of time for business stuff in my 30's.

If you notice that both of these explanations were 'positives' so to speak, you should be looking at suggestions from your parts that will be in your best interest. Just partying for partying sake wouldn't be useful for example, it was more that I would be missing the memories and potentially losing friends which was a somewhat valid point.

Then it is about having a negotiation session to see if you can resolve this conflicting chatter among these parts. Try to assess what each is doing for you and see if you can come to some agreement. For me I decided that the hardworking business side of me ultimately had my best interests at heart and should be listened to most.

However I came to a trade off. My fun loving part agreed that I could still go out with friends for one big night a month to let off some steam and help retain friendships and relationships but that I would put off any major leisure travel until I'd reached certain benchmarks in my business. My entrepreneurial side agreed to this as 100% work wasn't ultimately healthy for me.

Finally when you have come to some agreement regarding the two conflicting parts, you want to thank them for their input before bringing your palms together to join them back as one within yourself. What you should find is that you start to feel much more at ease and much less conflicted and confused then you previously were. For me this gave me so much more peace of mind when pursuing my business goals in the early years and I'm so glad that I did this exercise at the time.

Again for you it might be something similar or something completely different. My intention here is to just give you an idea of the process as with all of the techniques I describe in this book. And whilst this is not a cut and dry NLP strategy (if there is such a thing) but rather a cognitive exercise I have found to be highly effective at resolving conflicting parts within me which is why I have included it here.